EASY PIANO SOLOS

Elton John

ISBN 978-1-61774-209-5

EXCLUSIVELY DISTRIBUTED BY

HAL•LEONARD®
CORPORATION

7777 W. BLUEMOUND RD. P.O. BOX 13819 MILWAUKEE, WI 53213

Visit Hal Leonard Online at
www.halleonard.com

BENNIE AND THE JETS

Words and Music by ELTON JOHN
and BERNIE TAUPIN

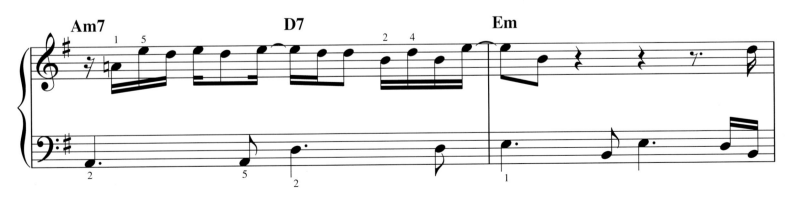

BLUE EYES

Words and Music by ELTON JOHN
and GARY OSBORNE

DANIEL

Words and Music by ELTON JOHN
and BERNIE TAUPIN

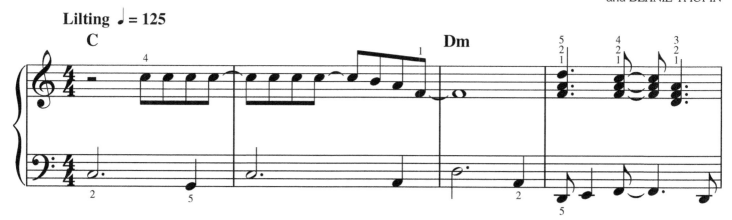

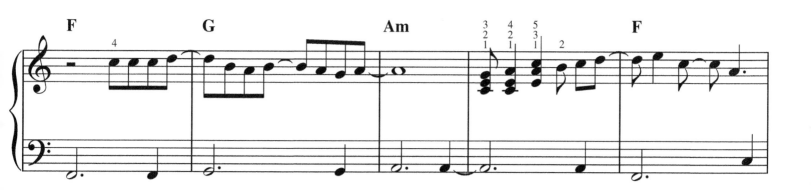

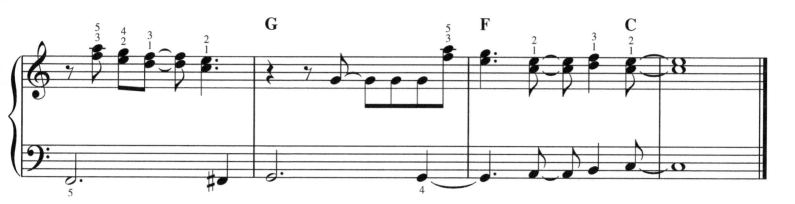

CAN YOU FEEL THE LOVE TONIGHT

from Walt Disney Pictures' THE LION KING

Music by Elton John
Lyrics by Tim Rice

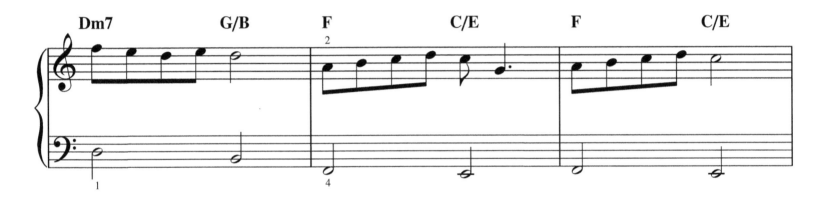

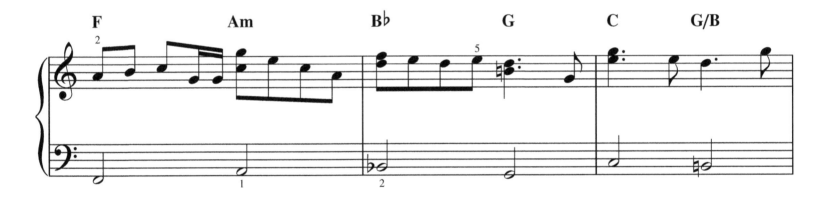

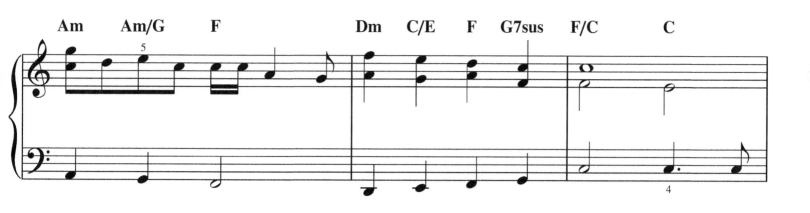

CANDLE IN THE WIND

Words and Music by ELTON JOHN
and BERNIE TAUPIN

Moderately

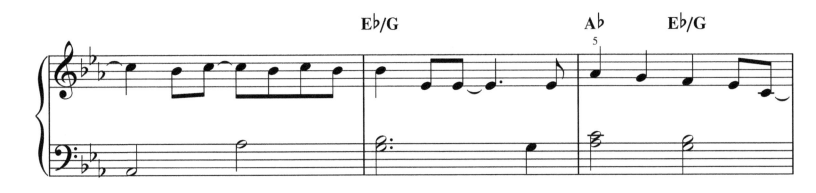

CROCODILE ROCK

Words and Music by ELTON JOHN
and BERNIE TAUPIN

Light Rock ♩ = 134

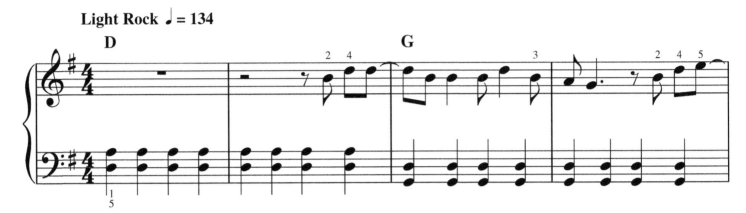

DON'T GO BREAKING MY HEART

Words and Music by CARTE BLANCHE
and ANN ORSON

DON'T LET THE SUN
GO DOWN ON ME

Words and Music by ELTON JOHN
and BERNIE TAUPIN

ELECTRICITY

from BILLY ELLIOT

Music by ELTON JOHN
Lyrics by LEE HALL

With emotion ♩ = 68

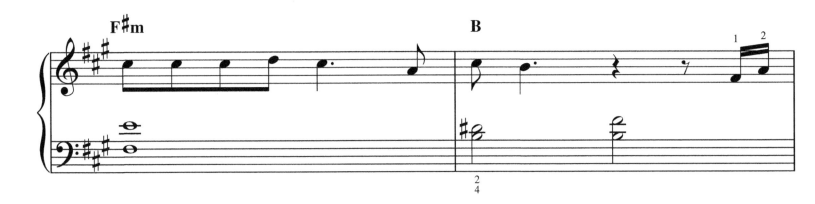

GOODBYE YELLOW BRICK ROAD

Words and Music by ELTON JOHN
and BERNIE TAUPIN

Slow Swing ♩ = 80

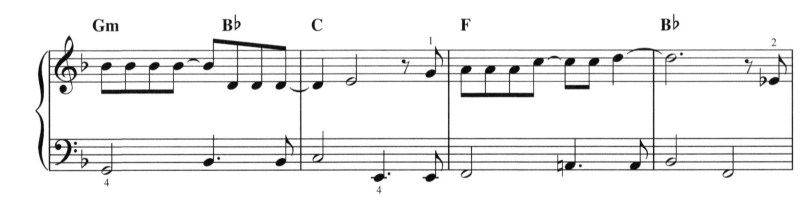

I GUESS THAT'S WHY THEY CALL IT THE BLUES

Words and Music by ELTON JOHN,
BERNIE TAUPIN and DAVEY JOHNSTONE

I WANT LOVE

Words and Music by ELTON JOHN
and BERNIE TAUPIN

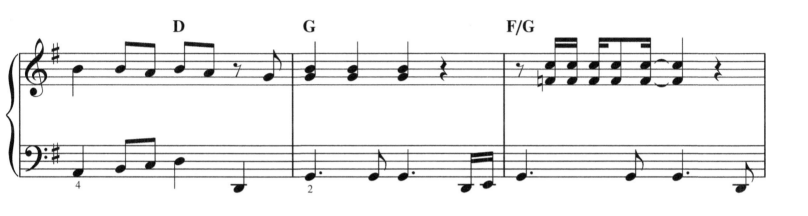

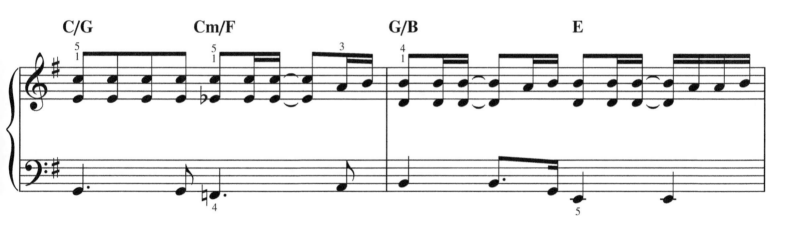

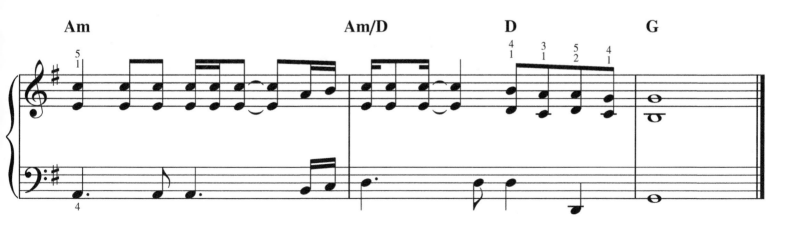

I'M STILL STANDING

Words and Music by ELTON JOHN
and BERNIE TAUPIN

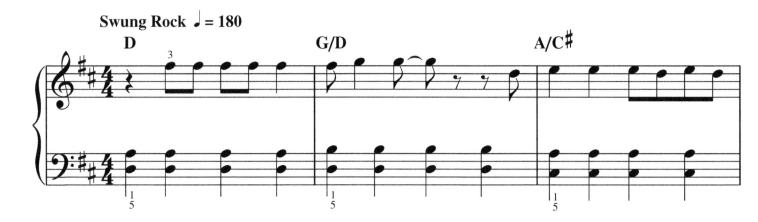

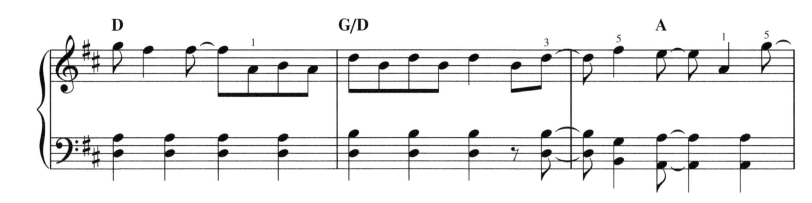

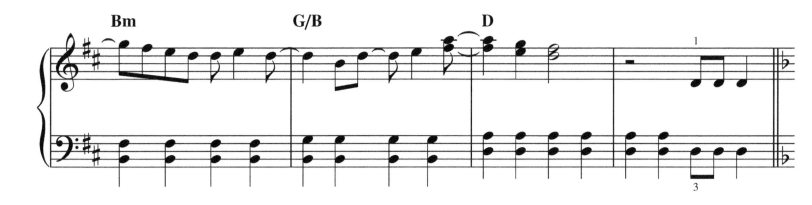

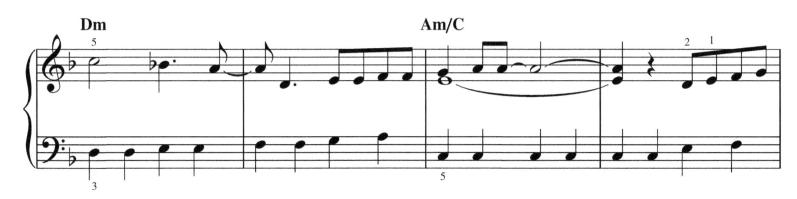

NIKITA

Words and Music by ELTON JOHN
and BERNIE TAUPIN

THE ONE

Words and Music by ELTON JOHN
and BERNIE TAUPIN

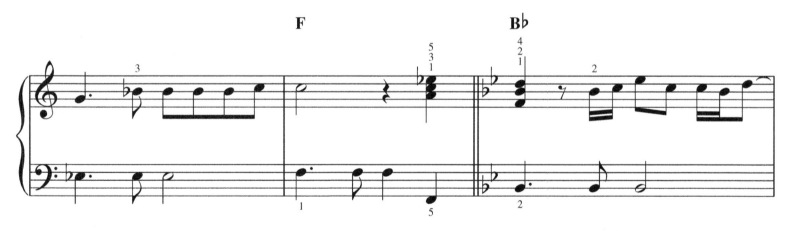

PASSENGERS

Words and Music by ELTON JOHN,
BERNIE TAUPIN, DAVEY JOHNSTONE
and PHINEAS McHIZE

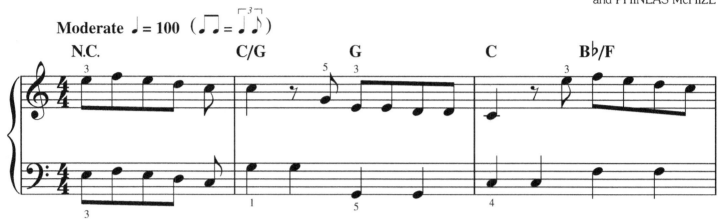

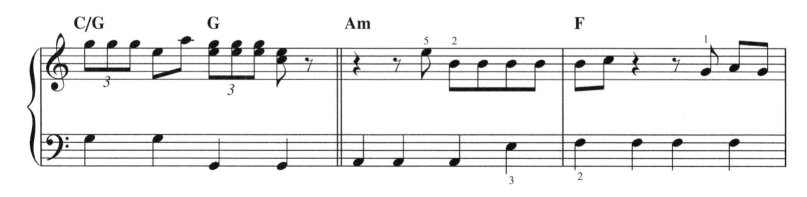

ROCKET MAN
(I Think It's Gonna Be a Long Long Time)

Words and Music by ELTON JOHN
and BERNIE TAUPIN

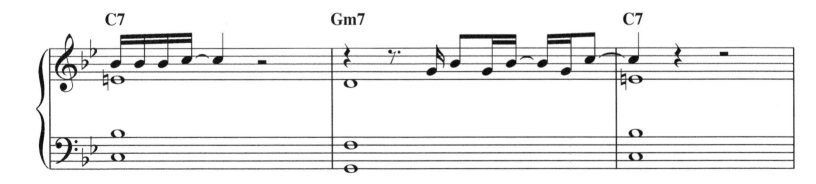

33

SACRIFICE

Words and Music by ELTON JOHN
and BERNIE TAUPIN

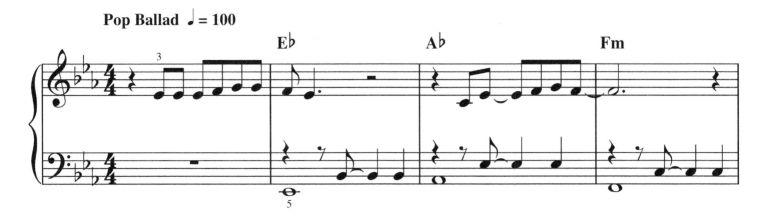

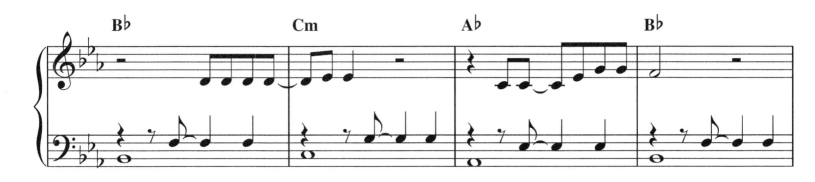

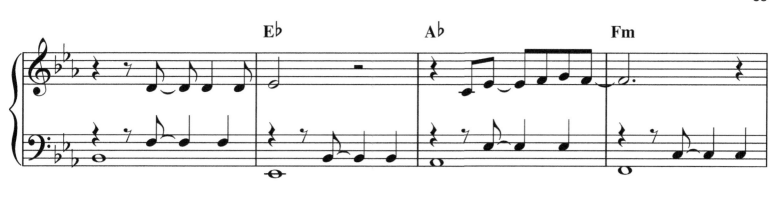

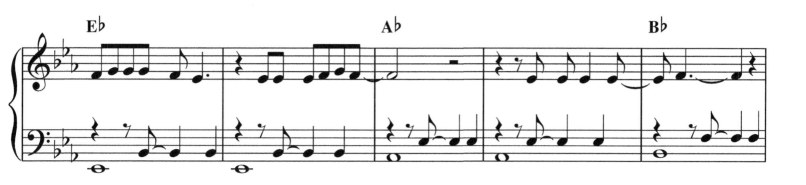

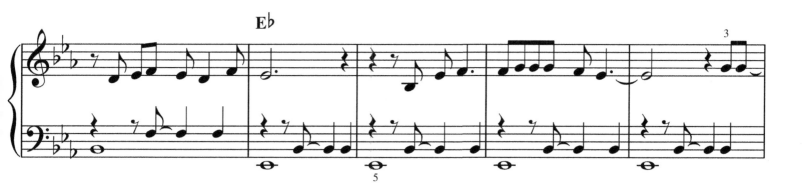

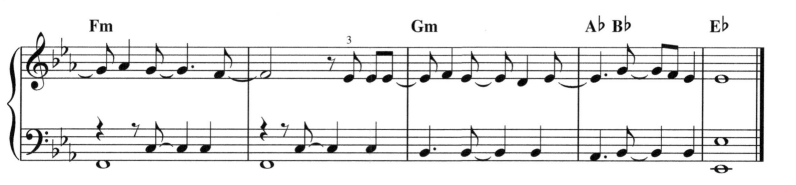

SAD SONGS
(Say So Much)

Words and Music by ELTON JOHN
and BERNIE TAUPIN

Moderate Blues ♩ = 100

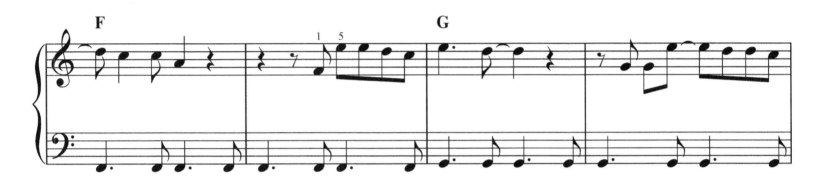

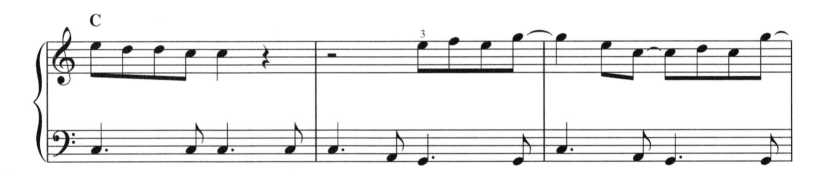

SATURDAY NIGHT'S ALRIGHT
(For Fighting)

Words and Music by ELTON JOHN
and BERNIE TAUPIN

Funky groove ♩ = 148

SOMETHING ABOUT THE WAY
YOU LOOK TONIGHT

Words and Music by ELTON JOHN
and BERNIE TAUPIN

SORRY SEEMS TO BE THE HARDEST WORD

Words and Music by ELTON JOHN
and BERNIE TAUPIN

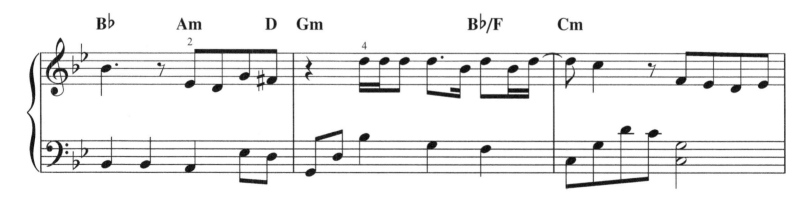

TINY DANCER

Words and Music by ELTON JOHN
and BERNIE TAUPIN

Slow, with rhythm ♩ = 74

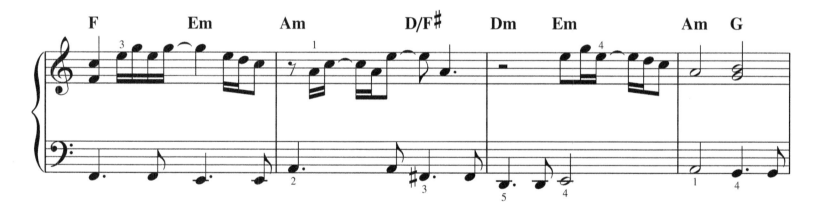

YOUR SONG

Words and Music by ELTON JOHN
and BERNIE TAUPIN

Slow, but pushing forward ♩ = 60

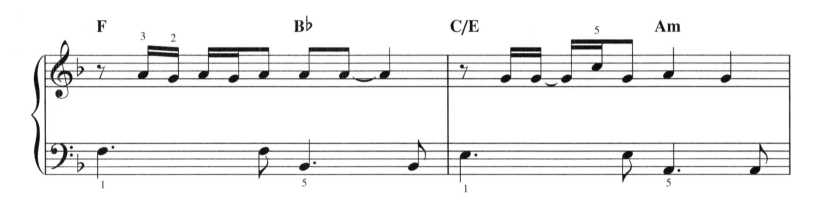

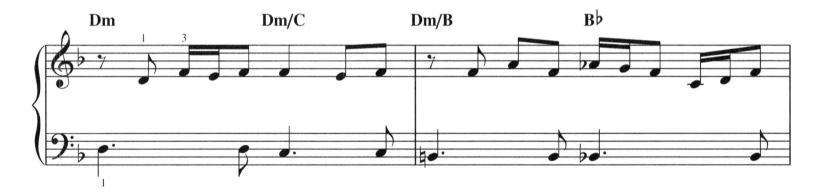

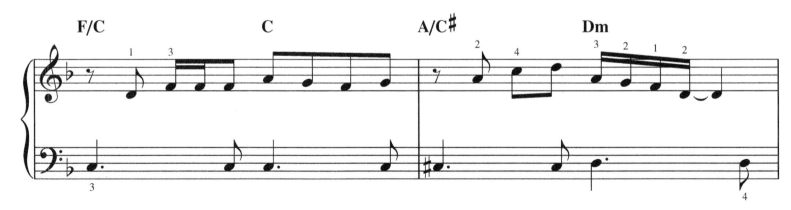